The INSIDE GUIDE

GLOBAL GEOGRAPHY

# Exploring the Geography of the Middle East and North Africa

By Heather Smore



Cavendish Square

Published in 2026 by Cavendish Square Publishing, LLC
2544 Clinton Street Buffalo, NY 14224



Website: cavendishsq.com



Disclaimer: Portions of this work were originally authored by Miriam Coleman and published as *The Geography of Southwest Asia and North Africa* (Explore the World). All new material this edition authored by Heather Smore.

All websites were available and accurate when this book was sent to press.

Cataloging-in-Publication Data

Names: Smore, Heather.
Title: Exploring the geography of the Middle East and North Africa / Heather Smore.
Description: Buffalo, NY : Cavendish Square Publishing, 2026. | Series: The inside guide: global geography | Includes glossary and index.
Identifiers: ISBN 9781502674289 (pbk.) | ISBN 9781502674296 (library bound) | ISBN 9781502674302 (ebook)
Subjects: LCSH: Middle East–Geography–Juvenile literature. | Africa, North–Geography–Juvenile literature. | Middle East–Juvenile literature. | Africa, North–Juvenile literature.
Classification: LCC DS44.96 S66 2026 | DDC 915.6–dc23

Editor: Katie Kawa
Designer: Deanna Lepovich

The photographs in this book are used by permission and through the courtesy of: Cover AFZAL KHAN MAHEEN/Shutterstock.com; p. 4 magr80/Shutterstock.com; p. 6 bodrumsurf/Shutterstock.com; p. 7 Nastya Smirnova RF/Shutterstock.com; p. 8 eyetravelphotos/Shutterstock.com; p. 9 frantic00/Shutterstock.com; p. 10 Sabbir Digital/Shutterstock.com; p. 12 (top) skostep/Shutterstock.com; p. 12 (bottom) givaga/Shutterstock.com; p. 13 Ayman shalaby/Shutterstock.com; p. 14 NASA images/Shutterstock.com; p. 15 Slim Segi/Shutterstock.com; p. 16 TTstudio/Shutterstock.com; pp. 18 (top), 29 (left) muratart/Shutterstock.com; p. 18 (bottom) Efired/Shutterstock.com; p. 19 Mistervlad/Shutterstock.com; p. 20 Framalicious/Shutterstock.com; pp. 21, 22 Anas-Mohammed/Shutterstock.com; p. 24 (top) TAJ Photoz/Shutterstock.com; p. 24 (bottom) John Wreford/Shutterstock.com; p. 25 Hussain Warraich/Shutterstock.com; p. 27 Fitria Ramli/Shutterstock.com; p. 28 (graphic organizer) Fireofheart/Shutterstock.com; p. 28 (top left and center) Oasis World/Shutterstock.com; p. 28 (top right) Katty2016/Shutterstock.com; p. 28 (bottom left) Dasha Kurinna/Shutterstock.com; p. 28 (bottom right) MyPro/Shutterstock.com; p. 29 (right) PVRM/Shutterstock.com.



CPSIA compliance information: Batch #CSCSQ26: For further information contact Cavendish Square Publishing LLC at 1-877-980-4450.

Printed in the United States of America

# CONTENTS

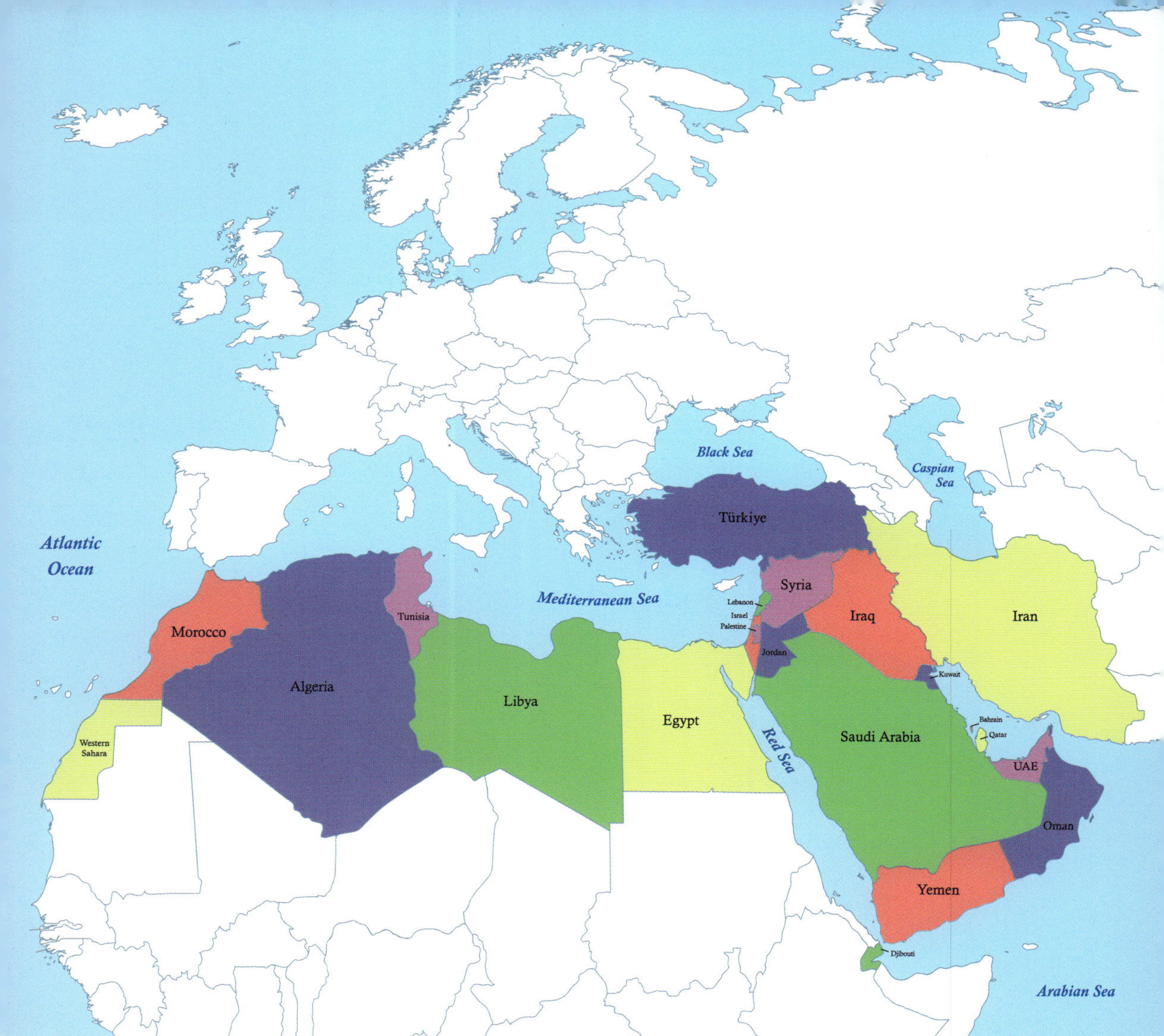


**This map shows the nations that are commonly considered part of the Middle East and North Africa. Different international organizations have different definitions of this region that include different countries. For example, some groups do not include Türkiye, but many do.**

# ANCIENT AND MODERN

Chapter One

The countries of Southwest Asia and North Africa are often grouped together as part of a region called the Middle East or the Middle East and North Africa (sometimes shortened to MENA). This region has ancient roots. It is the birthplace of three major world religions—Judaism, Christianity, and Islam—and countless technological innovations. It is also a region of great importance in current global politics and has many modern cities. This combination of the ancient and the modern makes this region a truly fascinating one to study.

> **Fast Fact**
>
> Many Middle Eastern countries are found on the Asian continent, which is part of a supercontinent called Eurasia. This giant landmass is home to the continents of Europe and Asia. In fact, the nation of Türkiye has land on both continents.

## Two Important Rivers

Ancient history in this region can be traced back to life along two major rivers: the Tigris and the Euphrates. They originate, or begin, high in the mountains of Türkiye and flow nearly parallel to each other on their course through Syria and Iraq. In southern Iraq, the rivers join to become the

**The Euphrates River is shown here. Throughout the history of the Middle East, people have built canals and dams on the Tigris and Euphrates Rivers. This has changed their courses over time.**

**Fast Fact**

The Euphrates flows for about 1,740 miles (2,800.3 km). It is the longest river in western Asia. The Tigris comes in second, at about 1,180 miles (1,899 km).

Shatt al-Arab River, which forms the border between Iran and Iraq before flowing into the Persian Gulf.

These rivers allowed for the development of early civilizations. Ancient peoples could use their waters for **irrigation** in a dry region, and the fertile soil around them made agriculture possible.

## The Fertile Crescent

The ancient region of Mesopotamia developed between the Tigris and the Euphrates Rivers. Mesopotamia is a key part of the geographic area known as the Fertile Crescent. This is an arc of land that curves through

## CHANGING THE LAND

The impact humans can have on geography can be seen very clearly in the lands of the Fertile Crescent. As people developed more advanced irrigation projects and dams along the Tigris and Euphrates Rivers, the lands around the rivers became less fertile. By the beginning of the 21st century, 90 percent of the wetlands of the region had disappeared, turning more than 1,000 square miles (2,590 sq km) of fertile marshes into desert.

Some of these irrigation projects have been a source of conflict in the region. For example, Türkiye has created a massive network of dams and canals along the rivers. This has taken water away from Iraq and Syria, creating **tension** between these countries.

parts of Iraq, Syria, Lebanon, Jordan, the Palestinian territories, Israel, Türkiye, and Iran, between the Mediterranean Sea and the Persian Gulf.

**Mesopotamia was home to ancient peoples such as the Sumerians, the Babylonians, and the Assyrians. Today, people can see the remains of these civilizations, such as the ruins shown here, in parts of the Middle East.**

> ## Fast Fact
> Baghdad, the capital city of Iraq, was founded along the banks of the Tigris River in the 8th century CE.

Some experts also include Kuwait and Egypt's Nile River valley as part of the Fertile Crescent as well.

The Fertile Crescent got its name from the fertile soil of the area. This allowed for permanent agricultural settlements, which became civilizations.

## Uniting the Region

In ancient times, many different civilizations rose and fell across the lands of the Middle East and North Africa. Then, in the 7th century CE, a new religion spread across the region and came to define the **culture** of many of its nations. The religion of Islam began in today's Saudi Arabia and was brought to other parts of the region—and later, the world—through trade and conquest. Today, most of the Middle East and North Africa shares the Muslim faith.

**Mosques, such as the one shown here, are found throughout the Middle East and North Africa today. These are buildings where Muslims gather to pray.**

In the 14th century, many of these lands came under the control of the Ottoman Empire. This united the region politically, although many diverse cultural groups still existed.

## Dividing the Region

Following the collapse of the Ottoman Empire in World War I (1914-1918), the European powers on the winning side of the war carved up the empire's lands. New borders were often drawn without regard to traditional boundaries or **access** to water sources, creating tensions that are still felt in the region today.

The European powers even influenced the name of the region. They called it the Middle East to **distinguish** it from the "Far East," which referred to East Asia. This way of looking at the world is Eurocentric, which means it describes the regions from a Western European point of view. However, the name stuck, even within the region itself.

**Although many people in the Middle East and North Africa, such as those shown here in the United Arab Emirates, share the Muslim faith and the Arabic language, there is still a lot of diversity among the people of the region. The lands they live on are also diverse.**

When people think of the geography of the Middle East and North Africa, they often think of a scene like this one, with long stretches of empty deserts populated only by camels. However, while deserts are a major part of this region, there are also many other geographic features to explore.

# DEFINING GEOGRAPHIC FEATURES

Chapter Two

Although the Tigris and Euphrates Rivers first attracted settlers to the Middle East, they are not the only geographic features that have shaped life in this region throughout its history. The nations of the Middle East and North Africa are home to snow-capped mountains, coral reefs, major bodies of water, and vast deserts.

## The Sands of the Sahara

Deserts make up a large part of this region's landscape. This includes the Sahara—the world's largest hot desert. It covers nearly a third of Africa and forms a distinct division between the countries of North Africa and the rest of the continent.

The Sahara, with a name that comes from the Arabic word for desert, covers approximately 3.6 million square miles (9.3 million sq km). It stretches between the Atlantic Ocean to the west, the Red Sea to the east, the Mediterranean Sea and Atlas Mountains to the north, and the grasslands of the African savanna to the south.

**Fast Fact**

The Sahara has more than 90 major oases, or fertile pockets of land.

**Sand dunes such as the ones shown here make up a large part of the Sahara. It is very hard for things to live in this hot, dry place—including humans.**

## The Nile River

The Sahara is a major part of the geography of North Africa, but this region is more than just dry desert. In fact, it is home to the world's longest river. The Nile River flows 4,130 miles (6,646.6 km) north from its sources in Ethiopia and central Africa into the Mediterranean Sea.

With fertile banks fed by annual floods, the Nile has played a vital role in agriculture and transportation in North Africa since the founding of the ancient Egyptian civilization. Today, around 95 percent of the population of Egypt lives near this river, making it one of the most important geographic features in the region.

**The Egyptian capital of Cairo (*shown here*) developed along the banks of the Nile River.**

## A Salty Sea

Another important body of water in the Middle East and North Africa is the Red Sea. This sea is a long, narrow body of salt water that divides the continents of Asia and Africa. The Red Sea is about 1,200 miles (1,931.2 km) long, and its widest point is 190 miles (305.8 km) across.

**Fast Fact**

The Red Sea is considered one of the saltiest seas in the world.

An inlet of the Indian Ocean, the Red Sea has served as an important trade route for thousands of years, dating back to the time of the ancient Egyptians. Even today, it remains one of the world's busiest waterways.

**The Red Sea is home to coral reefs such as the one shown here.**

**Fast Fact**

The Dead Sea, which borders Jordan, Israel, and Palestinian lands, is a salt lake in the Middle East. It is the lowest point on Earth that is not underwater, with an elevation of 1,412 feet (431 m) below sea level at its shores.

## The Largest Peninsula

The Middle East is home to the world's largest **peninsula**: the Arabian Peninsula, also known as Arabia. The coasts of Arabia do have some fertile agricultural regions, but most of the peninsula has a dry climate. The Arabian Desert, an **extension** of the Sahara, covers most of the peninsula.

The Arabian Peninsula contains Saudi Arabia (which covers about 80 percent of the peninsula), Yemen, Oman, Qatar, Kuwait, and the United Arab Emirates. All these countries, except for Yemen, are on the Persian Gulf (also called the Arabian Gulf). This location has provided them with important ports for trade and large reserves of oil.

Shown here is what the Arabian Peninsula looks like from space. Over millions of years, the Arabian and African tectonic plates separated, creating the Red Sea and forming the shape of the Arabian Peninsula. Tectonic plates are large, moving pieces of Earth's crust.

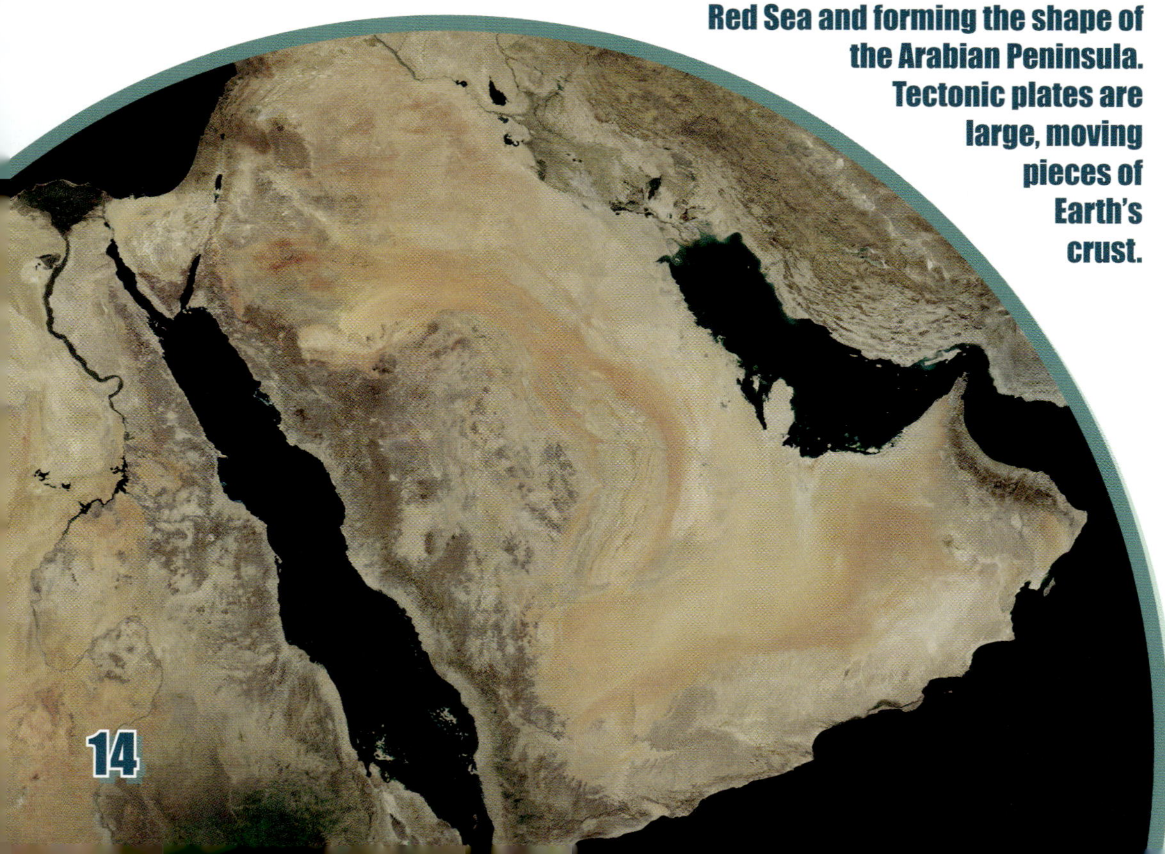

# EXPLORING THE EMPTINESS

The largest continuous, or unbroken, stretch of sand in the world can be found in the Arabian Desert. The Rub' al-Khali, which means "Empty Quarter" in Arabic, takes up more than a quarter of Saudi Arabia's land area and includes parts of Yemen, Oman, and the United Arab Emirates as well. Stretching over an area of about 250,000 square miles (647,497 sq km), this is one of the most arid, or extremely dry, places on the planet. However, it has one very important resource: oil. In fact, it contains the world's largest oil field.

The Empty Quarter, which is shown here, is one of the most inhospitable places on Earth. This means it's nearly impossible to live there.

**The Middle East has many major cities that attract people for work and for fun. Dubai (*shown here*) is a city in the United Arab Emirates that millions of people visit each year for its shopping, dining, and fancy hotels.**

# IMPORTANT CITIES

Chapter Three

Scattered throughout the desert areas and fertile river valleys of the Middle East and North Africa are a number of major cities. Many of these cities have ancient roots, so visitors can find both historic treasures and modern attractions. As these cities—such as Baghdad in Iraq, Damascus in Syria, and Mecca in Saudi Arabia—grew over centuries, they developed their own **architecture**, foods, and lifestyles.

## The City of Cairo

The most populated city in North Africa is Egypt's capital, Cairo. The city itself has a population of around 10 million people, and more than 20 million people live in the greater metropolitan area, which includes surrounding lands.

> **Fast Fact**
>
> Mecca is known as the birthplace of Islam. All Muslims are required to travel to Mecca at least once in their lifetime, as long as they are healthy enough and financially able to make the trip.

Modern Cairo was founded more than 1,000 years ago along the banks of the Nile River, although ancient Egyptians had settled in the area around 2000 BCE. Today, Cairo is a huge, vibrant city combining modern buildings and ancient monuments.

**Cairo's population is expanding so rapidly that close to a million people now live in and around the shrines and tombs of al-Qarafah (*shown here*). Also called the City of the Dead, this group of ancient cemeteries, or burial places, lies on the eastern edge of the city.**

The most famous ancient site is the pyramids of Giza, which are found on the southwestern edge of Cairo's metropolitan area.

## A Tour of Tehran

Iran is a powerful Middle Eastern nation, and its capital, Tehran, has a dramatic landscape. It reaches down from the Alborz mountains into the Dasht-e Kavir desert. Tehran is a young city, founded less than 250 years ago. However, settlements have existed in its general area for thousands of years. At the city's center, Old Tehran holds historic structures, but most of Tehran's buildings were built after the 1960s.

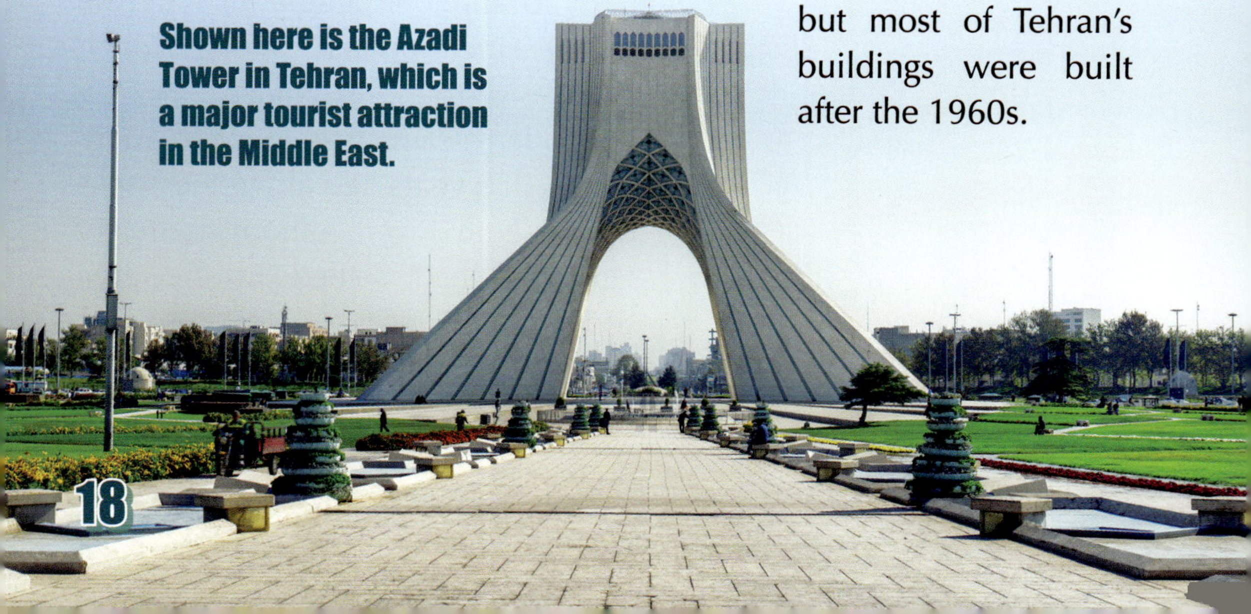

**Shown here is the Azadi Tower in Tehran, which is a major tourist attraction in the Middle East.**

As Iran's capital city, Tehran offers many job opportunities in government, service, and manufacturing. Nearly 10 million people live in this city, making it the largest city in Iran and one of the largest in the region.

**Fast Fact**

**The highest mountain peak in the Middle East is located in Iran. The height of Mount Damavand varies by source, but it is believed to be more than 18,400 feet (5,610 m) tall.**

## A City on Two Continents

Istanbul, Türkiye, is a very **unique** city because it is located on two continents. The city sits on both sides of the Bosporus strait, a waterway that is a geographic border between Europe and Asia. The Bosporus connects the Black Sea to the Mediterranean Sea through the Sea of Marmara. Istanbul contains Türkiye's largest seaport, and its bordering waters are a major route for ships carrying oil to Europe.

Although Türkiye's political capital is Ankara, Istanbul

**Hagia Sophia (*shown here*) is a mosque in Istanbul that was once a Christian church. Today, it is one of the most famous buildings in the Middle East.**

## Fast Fact

Türkiye is located at the meeting point of tectonic plates, which means earthquakes happen frequently as these plates move and touch each other. In February 2023, an earthquake near the border between Türkiye and Syria killed more than 50,000 people.

is considered the cultural and financial heart of the country. Around 20 percent of Turkey's population lives there, which is around 15 million people.

## A Sacred City

Jerusalem is more than just the capital of the nation of Israel. It is considered a sacred, or very holy, city in Christianity, Judaism, and Islam. They are the world's most prominent, or well-known, monotheistic religions. These are belief systems based on the idea of one God instead of many gods.

Parts of Jerusalem contain monuments that are important for followers of each of these religions. Notable structures include the Jews' Western Wall, the Muslims' Dome of the Rock shrine and Al-Aqsa Mosque, and the Christians' Church of the Holy Sepulchre. These structures represent thousands of years of history.

**Jerusalem (*shown here*) is an ancient city built on hills that are around 2,500 feet (762 m) high.**

# A REGION AT WAR

Israel is officially a Jewish state in a region where most people are Muslim. In the decades before Israel became a nation in 1948, the land was part of a territory called Palestine that was controlled by the Ottoman Empire and then Great Britain. The new Jewish state forced out Arab Palestinians living in Israel.

Today, Palestinians govern the Gaza Strip, a small ribbon of coastland between Israel and Egypt, and the West Bank, which lies between Israel and the west bank of the Jordan River. Conflicts between Israelis and Palestinians happen often in this region, with the most recent one breaking out in 2023.

According to many sources, around 50,000 Palestinians were killed between the beginning of the latest conflict with Israel in 2023 and the start of 2025. Shown here is the aftermath of an Israeli airstrike on Palestinian territory.

One way people have adapted to the geography of the Middle East and North Africa is by growing crops that can survive in the sandy soil and hot climate of the region. For example, date palms, such as those shown here, grow throughout the region.

# ADAPTING TO THE LAND

Chapter Four

The Middle East and North Africa make up a region known for being extremely dry and hot. It can be hard for things to grow and people to thrive in such a challenging landscape. However, over thousands of years, people have learned to adapt to the extremes of this region's geography. These adaptations combine old traditions with new technologies.

## Dealing with the Heat

The hot climate of the Middle East and North Africa calls for special adaptations for all the living things that call this region home. For humans, it's created a need for clothing that allows people to stay comfortable in extreme heat. This is why men and women in this region often wear loose robes and long **tunics** or dresses that allow air to move around the body. Head coverings also protect people from the sun, wind, and sand.

Keeping homes cool is another challenge. Traditional architecture used features such as courtyards to keep cool air flowing through buildings, but most modern buildings use air conditioning systems.

Traditional Arab clothing serves an important purpose. It keeps people cool and protects them from the strong rays of the desert sun.

## Where Is the Water?

Life in the Middle East and North Africa is closely connected to the region's very limited water resources. The high temperatures of this region cause rivers and lakes to evaporate, and low levels of rainfall mean freshwater sources are not easily **replenished**.

Climate change is creating new challenges for the Middle East and North Africa, causing increased droughts, declining rainfall, and greater water evaporation from higher temperatures. This is expected to make it even harder to find water sources in this dry region.

## Fast Fact

The Middle East and North Africa as a region has 6 percent of the world's population but only 1 percent of the world's fresh water, making it the most water-scarce region on Earth.

Water **scarcity** has led to food shortages, disease outbreaks, and violent conflicts, so combating it is necessary for the future of this region. One common method used to provide enough water for people's needs is desalinization, also called desalination. This process uses nearby seas and oceans and removes the salt from the water to create fresh water.

## The Importance of Oil

One way people have adapted to their geography throughout history is by making the most of the natural resources around them, and the people of this region are no exception. The most important natural resource in this region

## Fast Fact

In 1908, oil was discovered in Iran. This is the first known discovery of oil in the Middle East.

**An oil rig, such as the one shown here, is a device for taking oil from the ground. It is a common sight in the Middle East.**

# OIL AND CLIMATE CHANGE

Although oil continues to be an important export, or good sold to other countries, for some Middle Eastern nations, many countries around the world are trying to use less of it. This is because oil is a **fossil fuel**, and fossil fuels play a part in climate change.

The burning of fossil fuels releases gases that trap heat in Earth's atmosphere, warming up the planet and changing the climate over time. In the Middle East and North Africa, climate change is causing the extreme dryness and heat to get worse.

> **Fast Fact**
>
> Saudi Arabia produces more oil than any other nation in the Middle East and North Africa. The only country in the world that produces more oil is the United States.

is petroleum, or oil. Over the last century, oil rigs have multiplied across the Arabian Peninsula.

Oil has driven the economy of the region, making many Middle Eastern nations very wealthy. In 1960, the oil-rich Middle Eastern countries of Saudi Arabia, Iran, Iraq, and Kuwait, along with Venezuela, formed the Organization of the Petroleum Exporting Countries (OPEC), which is a major force in the global economy.

## Finding Solutions

The geography of the Middle East and North Africa has challenged the people of this region since settlement began in ancient times.

Today, those challenges have become more severe, or extreme, because of climate change and the changing of fertile land to desert because of agricultural overuse.

Competition for scarce water resources in the region has led to intense conflict, yet the need to find solutions to the problem could be an opportunity for cooperation in the future. The people of this region have found ways to work with the land for thousands of years, and working with each other is one way they can continue to adapt to their unique geography.

**Flag Plaza in Qatar (*shown here*) celebrates the spirit of cooperation and unity necessary to keep this region moving forward as it has throughout history. It features more than 100 flags from countries and organizations around the world.**

# THE MIDDLE EAST AND NORTH AFRICA BY THE NUMBERS

## Largest Country (by Area)

Algeria:
919,600 square miles
(2,381,753 sq km)

## Most Populated Country

Egypt:
115 million people

## Smallest Country (by Area)

Bahrain:
305 square miles
(790 sq km)

## Highest Point

Mount Damavand:
approximately
18,400 feet (5,610 m)

## Longest River

Nile: 4,130 miles
(6,646.6 km)

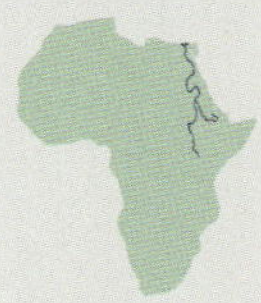

# THINK ABOUT IT!

1. How did European interference in the Middle East and North Africa create problems in the region that are still being felt today?

2. Why do you think the Nile River has been an important geographic feature in North Africa since ancient times?

3. Why do you think the creation of the nation of Israel was—and remains—a major source of tension in the Middle East?

4. Why do you think the connection between fossil fuels and climate change is especially challenging for Middle Eastern countries to deal with?

# GLOSSARY

**access:** The ability to use or have something.

**architecture:** The art or science of designing and building structures, especially ones that can be lived in.

**culture:** The beliefs and ways of life of a certain group of people.

**distinguish:** To know or point out the difference between things.

**extension:** A part forming an addition to something.

**fossil fuel:** A fuel—such as coal, oil, or natural gas—that is formed in the earth from dead plants or animals.

**irrigation:** The supplying of water to land by man-made means.

**peninsula:** A piece of land surrounded by water on three sides.

**replenish:** To fill or build up again.

**scarcity:** The state of having a very small supply of something.

**tension:** A state in which people, groups, or countries disagree with and feel anger toward each other.

**tunic:** A piece of clothing that is like a shirt that reaches to the knees.

**unique:** Special or different from anything else.

# FIND OUT MORE

## Books

Doeden, Matt. *Travel to Israel*. Minneapolis, MN: Lerner Publications, 2022.

London, Martha. *The Middle East*. Lake Elmo: MN: Focus Readers, 2021.

Vink, Amanda. *The History and Government of Southwest Asia and North Africa*. Buffalo, NY: PowerKids Press, 2021.

## Websites

***National Geographic Kids*: Iran Country Profile**
*kids.nationalgeographic.com/geography/countries/article/iran*
Visitors to this website can find facts about the Middle Eastern nation of Iran.

**Timeline of Ancient Egypt**
*www.britishmuseum.org/learn/schools/ages-7-11/ancient-egypt/timeline-ancient-egypt*
The British Museum provides a timeline that students can use to learn more about the ancient civilization that developed along the Nile River in Egypt.

**UNICEF Youth: Child-Friendly Guide to the Gaza and Israel Crisis**
*www.unicef.org.au/unicef-youth/making-sense-of-emergencies/youth-israel-palestine-crisis*
The international children's organization known as UNICEF breaks down the conflict between Israelis and Palestinians in a way that is easy for young people to understand.

# INDEX